# LEA

# TRUTH

## 8 STEPS TO YOUR MOST AUTHENTIC SELF IN YOUR LEADERSHIP JOURNEY

*Enjoy your read* :)

*Rosa*

# Rasie Bamigbade

# LEAD IN YOUR TRUTH

## 8 Steps to Becoming Your Most Authentic Self in Your Leadership Journey

# Advance Reader's

# Praise

I have read many leadership books, but I have not came across a book like 'Lead in your truth' by Rasie Bamigbade. This book provides leaders the opportunity to discover how they can effortlessly manifest the quality of a good leader and how they can implement leadership roles in a stress-free environment. The structure of the book is unique. It gives value and clarity to the reader. The author raises awareness of the need of practicing authentic leadership, and how the practices translates to increase in productivity. The book also layout a clear process every leader can easily adopt to improve on their performance and team output. I recommend it for everyone in a leadership position.

**~ Dr. Francis Mbunya**
**Founder & CEO, Authors Path Academy**

Lead in your truth is a wonderful read for leaders who wants to effect the necessary changes in their quest to succeed. This book enlightened me on the big lie of being busy in the workplace often told by leaders and how it can create negative narratives on followers. Moreover, I love the simplicity of the whole book and the positive mindset it will give readers all around the world.

**~ Alpha Bakarr Timbo**
**Personal Results Coach – ABT Coaching**

"Lead in your truth" gives great insight into the author's path to leadership. Through her story, she gives leaders tangible tools and actionable suggestions to help them achieve their leadership goals authentically. A great read for those who are struggling to enter into management or push through to the next level in their career.

**~Rikka Bouseh**
**Vice President, HR & Diversity, Equity & Inclusion**
**~ Evol Strategies**

"Rasie's story, experience, knowledge and framework expressed in her book are proof that leadership definitely starts from within. This book is a golden mine for all leaders who want to optimize their leadership skills."

**~Fabienne Raphaël,**
**Business Coach for High Achievers**

# Dedication

This book is dedicated to present and future leaders. Leaders that look for ways to add value in their journey and are always striving to make the experience enjoyable for the ones that look up to them. I see you and can relate to your passion, hard work and non-stop persistence to pave the way for the ones to come. You are important and valued. Do not stop and keep the faith. Your work counts even on days when it doesn't seem like it. You've got this. Keep leading with your heart and in your truth.

# Table of Content

# Chapter 1

$\blacklozenge$———————•———————$\blacklozenge$

# Find Your True Value in Your Leadership Path

**M**ost leaders try different things to be effective in addressing problems. Sometimes these problems get you overwhelmed, frustrated, confused, and anxious. Imagine you have tried it all and are still not getting the results you desire. For most leaders, this is unfortunately a normal state in leadership. As a leadership coach, I have witnessed many of those who come to me to seek help express that they are overwhelmed, frustrated and exhausted in their roles as leaders. Why are they overwhelmed? You might ask. One of those who I have helped had worked in an organization for decades and needed to work with a coach to simplify things and raise the accountability bar. Another leader who worked with me was tired of being stuck in the same place and making the same mistakes repeatedly.

There is always a lot to do when you are leading a team. The pressure can push you to a point where you no longer care as much and are willing to compromise your values. Before you reach that point, my advice for you is to seek support and guidance from a mentor, coach, or an accountability partner. When you have tried different things to solve a problem without getting results, it can seem like the world is moving forward and you are stuck and can't get out.

I deliver the following results for each of my clients through my Jumpstart Process. For an ideal client to be the right fit for my process and approach, you have to be motivated, committed and ready to do the work. It might be simple to read that and say, "Yes, I am an ideal client." But first, ask yourself the following questions:

- When things went tough in the past, did I run the other way or rely on things to suppress the pain?

- When no one is watching, do I perform as if someone is watching?

- Am I willing to let go of activities that don't add value to my mind, work, and family?

Your answers tell me if you are motivated, committed and ready to do the work. Any change takes time, energy and a high level of discipline to sustain it and keep elevating.

## CLARITY IS KEY

When it is clear that you are ready to transform your leadership journey, you need to start with self-talk and consistency. These are key factors that can help you improve other areas in your leadership journey. How you talk to yourself will translate to how you talk to your teams. I am a firm believer in positive self-talk; I am not talking about just thinking positively but being very mindful of the words we used to form our thoughts, especially when things go wrong.

I have come across leaders who struggle to sleep at night because of the destructive self-talk they were so used to before they started working with me. It is unhealthy and only keeps you stuck and unproductive. Consistency applies to all areas of our lives. When you decide to be consistent in transforming your leadership journey in one area, you can expect to keep adding that skill to other areas of your lives. Consistency is a powerful skill, and I think everyone should invest time and energy in building this skill. In my experience, when I got consistent in many areas of my life, I had to keep going to keep my consistency scale balanced. Balance is key in my lifestyle.

Consistency and self-talk are some of the key factors I used in helping leaders through my Jumpstart Process. The results of working with me through my Jumpstart Process include:

- Empowered to Speak up
- Conflict Management Resolution
- Creating Time
- Stretched Mindset
- Clarity of your leadership Style

These are results I have reached for myself and I have delivered to others I have worked with. Let's start with 'empowered to speak up.' Many leaders can and do speak up. The question is, do you do so emotionally or constructively? Do you do it respectfully or do you do it to prove a point? Do you only speak up when the bosses are around, and you want to be seen? Are you speaking up for the greater good? These are questions that tell me where exactly you are in your leadership journey. I do not only help the people I work with become empowered to speak up, but also gear them towards speaking up for the greater good. To speak up for a cause that is bigger than them. Most times, it can be for your teams, community, family, or peers.

## DEALING WITH CONFLICT WITH SELF AND OTHERS

Conflict Management is something we have all struggled with within ourselves or with others or both. The thing with conflicts is that you can decide if you would manage it or not. However, you have to understand that conflicts do not just go away naturally. If you fail to address a conflicting situation, it stays there until something similar happens and more fuel is added to the old conflict. At this point emotions start to boil over again and rekindled the conflict. In a matter of time, that unresolved conflict can develop into resentment, anger, sadness or lack of accountability. It can create unhappiness towards the company you work for/with, people or ourselves. Not managing a conflict can also decrease morale, teamwork, and increase turnover. People might not like you as a leader when you have those tough conflict management conversations, but with time, they would understand why you did what you did and respect you. I have experienced this and so have many other people I have coached. My goal is to empower leaders to solve any conflict with zero hesitation. Managing conflict is not always about you as an individual, it is about you as the leader taking accountability and creating a better environment for everyone that you lead. It is about your team and then, you. Conflict management can take time; let's talk about the next result I deliver for each of my clients.

The lie I hear from many leaders is, I don't have enough time in a day. I said this too. It is a lie. We all have 24hrs and when we become present and do the work that needs to be done, we not only have time, but we have extra time to do the things that we love to do when we are not working. I walk each person who works with me through the process of taking inventory, reflecting and creating time. It is an uncomfortable process, but it works. I have had a few leaders resist the implementation of the process because the process pushes each of them out of their comfort zone. I think leadership should focus on how we can continue to stretch out of our comfort zone. When we stretch, we inspire our teams to stretch as well. Creating time is the result I deliver to the leaders I have helped. It is a powerful gift, and you are in control of how you want to spend your time. Time is catching up to you instead of you catching up to it. Now, to the next result of my Jumpstart Process.

## YOUR PERCEPTION IS YOUR REALITY

How we think and the wording of our thoughts can make our leadership journey enjoyable or draining. How you see challenges, opportunities or wins is the first step towards knowing what work you need to do to enjoy your leadership journey.

How do you react when you are challenged? How do you feel when you fall short of hitting a target? Do you know an opportunity when you see it? Are you looking for opportunities in front, behind and beside you? Do you celebrate your wins, no matter how small or big? What is the response from your team if you were to ask these questions?

Leaders who have been in the same role for decades have mentored me. I found out that they keep doing the same thing, so they keep getting the same results and are content with no stretching. This approach worked for them in their leadership; I've always wanted more than that in my leadership journey. I didn't want to stay in the comfort zone. I wanted to help my team grow. Leaders that stay in their comfort zone, keep their teams there and their companies in the comfort zone. Guess what happens? You start to see tenured employees speaking negatively about the company and push out other employees that are not highly motivated themselves. Unfortunately, those employees usually have the potential to grow into great leaders.

## GETTING OUT OF YOUR COMFORT ZONE

I ask leaders uncomfortable questions when they come to me for help; it is to help them stretch their minds. I refer to different tools that would work best for each of my clients. I am continuously stretching my mind and loving it. As my passion builds, I help those who work with me build theirs too. And guess what? I am not doing it alone. I work weekly with a business coach. So, you don't have to do it alone; we reach our goals sooner and have fun in the process when we ask for help or seek help from a mentor or coach.

The next result is the clarity of your leadership style. We all have different leadership styles, and some things work for us and some not so much. Earlier in my leadership journey, I struggled in discovering, knowing and being confident in my leadership style. I admired many leadership styles. My mentors, peers, and my team inspired me in the way they lead. I wanted to be a little bit of everything I admired in each leader. What I discovered was that my leadership style does not have to specifically follow one style among the categories of leadership styles. Instead, I can be a little bit of everything. I became, and I am becoming what I admired in other leaders. This is me embracing my authenticity and leading the way I aspire to lead.

Knowing what my client admires and where they are at in their leadership journey, I help them lead in their style and build on that to add value to themselves, their teams, organizations, and businesses.

Imagine going through the transformation and applying it daily to your leadership journey and enjoying the process? Consistency and self-talk are key factors that can set the foundation for your transformation. The results I deliver through my

Jumpstart Process can transform leaders from being overwhelmed, frustrated, unhappy, and exhausted to being calm and clear on what work they need to do. The interesting part is that they also have fun in the process. The results I deliver help leaders become empowered to speak up, learn conflict management and resolution skills, learn how to create time, stretch their mindset and receive clarity on their leadership style.

# Chapter 2

———————◆———————

## Changing The Narratives

In my leadership journey, I had to develop the required skills to get the results that I had always longed for. In the beginning, I had a limiting belief that I would never climb the ladder and be in different management positions. I did not see myself ever becoming that person. Being black and a young woman has its challenges. How did I let go of this belief? What inspired me to not think that way? I remember speaking to one of my teachers in high school about how I couldn't be a manager. She encouraged me to keep working hard and move up as time goes by. When I walked away from that conversation, I developed the belief that I can be the first black female to become a manager at the time. The young, black females that have this limiting belief can be inspired and see/know that anything is possible. You start by believing that it is attainable. When I changed that narrative, I was unstoppable, and I got promoted quickly into different roles. I enjoyed every moment, and I enjoyed growing. This was a foundation for more growth in my leadership journey.

It took me over a decade to start and improve on my empowerment to speak up, conflict management, creating time, stretching my mind and clarity of my leadership style. Now, I deliver these results for each of my clients. I am successful in my leadership coaching because of my leadership experience with different teams, my diverse experiences in my personal life, combined with staying disciplined and persistent in looking for opportunities to grow and my high emotional intelligence.

I worked with leaders that were stuck and refused to look for ways to solve the problems in front of them. As a result, our teams stayed stuck or left the company. This got me going because I strongly believe that when I was not growing, I was holding my team and company back from tremendous growth. I felt very responsible for this. You can say that I am very driven and loyal to my teams, peers and leaders.

I believe that there is always a way through any problem, challenge or conflict. It is our responsibility as leaders to find a way through and solve the problems at hand. As you read about my leadership journey, remember that I did not do it alone. I decided to do the work to get the results, but I did not stop at that. My ambition fed my energy to keep striving in every moment.

I was empowered to speak up because my team depended on me to do so. Whether it is said or unsaid, that pushed me to do so respectfully and constructively. I would speak in front of my mirror to see what the receiver would see from my tone, body language and facial expressions. Perception is the reality for most people. I did not want to be referred to as the assertive black lady. I cared about how my message was being received. When I started to speak up, I gained credibility, and I improved on focusing on solutions and not just talk about the problem. I did this because it irritated me when my peers would just talk about the problems with no proposed solutions. We are in leadership roles to solve problems that will improve working conditions for our teams and help them grow into who they are to become in the process.

The next skill I built on to close the opportunity gap in my leadership role was conflict management. I went from only thinking of how I felt to imagining what the other person is feeling. It was all about how

I felt at first, and I caused myself pain with this approach. When I didn't want to stay stuck in that, I spoke to my mentor at the time about how I would improve on this skill. Collectively with their advice and my practice, I developed empathy for others regardless of how intense the conflict was. This was tough to do, and with time and focusing on understanding rather than being right, it got easier.

Another result I am very passionate about (and I love it when this is solved for each of my clients) is creating time. We all have 24hrs in one day, but yet many leaders say this quite often, "If I only have more time." We have time and it is right now. We need to solve the time management problem to better lead our lives and teams better. Do you work 60 hours a week and at the end of each day, you are just exhausted and can barely be present and hold a conversation with your loved ones? I was stuck in this state of time management. I prioritized work over everything, and so many areas suffered. First of all, I needed to do some inventory of the time I spent as if I was budgeting and looking to minimize my spending. I wanted to be more present at home and keep a balance. I take my clients through this inventory process to reach the result of creating time. Creating time comes with boundaries. Overtime, I discovered that I was teaching, coaching and following up more to delegate more and invest time in developing talent on my team. Time is very precious to me and I don't plan on wasting it. This drives my passion to help my clients do this for themselves.

Through the process of achieving these results in my leadership roles, I have stretched my mind and gained clarity about the leader I am becoming. Leading is a responsibility to not take lightly; we are influencing future leaders that look up to us and creating the future from what we are doing right now.

# Chapter 3

———————————————

## You Have a Gift, Use It

Leaders have a voice, the gift to inspire people and influence the path taken by the ones we lead; how we choose to take action with our voice, to inspire, and to be authentic is up to us. If you are not challenged each day, the question to ask is what am I doing? And how can I add value to what I am already doing? If you are stuck doing the same mistakes and not reaching your desired results, I am here to share with you steps you can start taking. Whether you work with a coach or mentor right now, this will add value. It is not a guarantee to your results, it is a guide to help you get there.

Leaders that have a plan to stay accountable move and grow at a faster speed and because they lead their lives effectively along with their teams, they get to enjoy the process. I am saying this from my experience and my observation of effective leaders.

Setting goals is a great place to start because it creates another level of accountability, ambition for growth, reflection and results in leadership.

Success teaches you to be responsible for continuous elevation by learning to be more effective than last year, month, week, day or/and moment. My definition of success is keeping my life balanced, building healthy relationships with myself and others, and helping others in the process.

The next key step is building on talent and people development. It is a great measurement of a leader's success in any organization, business and community.

How you show up for yourself and your team will make it or break it for you in your leadership journey. Showing up each day with integrity and remaining fully present says more about a great leader's actions than the words being said.

Taking care of yourself is a great place to start. I love helping my clients close this gap so they can be more effective in their work. Taking care of yourself involves being respectful to yourself, the people you interact with and the ones that look up to you. We have a responsibility to show up as role models in our leadership journey.

Keep believing in yourself because when you do, you inspire others to do the same. Imagine a world full of more people that believe in themselves and believe that they can be anything they want to be.

Did you know that leading with high emotional intelligence is necessary right now? Always be curious about why you respond the way you do when you are reacting to what you have done or what someone on your team has done. Our emotions can be a gift or can be detrimental to our success; ongoing learning of our emotional intelligence is a necessary factor in our growth and influence of others.

The last but not the least important step is conflict management. Learning how to manage conflict objectively is key when you are climbing the corporate ladder because one wrong move can be detrimental to your growth in your workplace. The steps I have shared can guide you in your journey to becoming a better leader. But working with a coach or a mentor can elevate your accountability level and move your progress at a faster speed.

# Chapter 4

—————————•—————————

## The Destination

Setting goals create greater levels of accountability, ambition for growth, reflection, and results in leadership. There are problems we are constantly faced with in leadership that we can solve on our own, and when it is our first encounter with such a problem, it could take longer to solve. The other option is to seek support and guidance from your mentor, an expert, or your coach.

Lack of either self-development, growth mindset or discipline makes it very tough for your vision to be clear and lived by you and your team. Imagine sharing what the goals are for your business or organization and each day, you see the results increasing and your team is pumped and excited. How awesome would that be? Sometimes, leaders are very dedicated to developing the talents of their team member but then, lack the same focus for their self-development. This can keep your team stuck and only growing to your limited potential. For this reason, some employees will leave your organization and seek growth somewhere else. It is a cycle that goes over and over with every new employee and yes, this can be exhausting for the leaders. Do you feel that, if what I just said resonated, you need the solution to fix this? The solution starts with our minds.

In 2013, I went from thinking I was already in a growth mindset to discovering that I had a huge opportunity to stretch that. I did not know the right word was "stretch" until this year when I opened a coffee shop in a remote location away from home. If this was not the right time to stretch, I wasn't going to ponder on when the right time was. I had to get to work right away. The weather was usually in extremes with lots of wind chills. I not only had to work with a new team, but I also had to make new friends and wake up one hour earlier than usual to warm up my car before I drove. Everything was new and some days were tougher than others, but my determination was tougher. I am always up for a challenge. What I was about to go through needed a new level of discipline from within to follow through if I wanted to reach my personal and professional goals.

## WHAT IS YOUR FOLLOW-THROUGH PLAN?

Follow up plan is key in self-development, growth mindset, and discipline. This can activate feedback and reflection to know and see the difference between then and now. How do you level up on your accountability? I always asked myself, does what I am doing right now contribute to my goals? Am I doing what I said I would do? These are examples of questions I would randomly stop and ask myself, especially when things got tough, and I wanted to go back to my comfort zone. Maybe I wanted to blame someone else or the weather or the traffic. There are so many things that we can hold on to as the reason why we didn't do what we were supposed to do. This may mean that you have to ask yourself, "Am I ready and committed to this growth process? Making reflection and feedback part of the process makes it more enjoyable, not only for you but also for your team.

The first thing I did was set clear goals with my team. When I thought it was clear, I had to be specific and clearer about the daily actions and targets. When I had not been clear on my personal goals in the past, I did not reach the results I wanted. I wasn't going to learn this twice in a new city, a new team, and on cold days. I made sure to include every person on my team. This meant that I had to work different schedules at the start of the month or work a double shift so that I can ensure everyone was getting the same information. This is the fun part; my team looked forward to this every month, and whether I wanted to do it or not, I had to. I had inspired them to be goal-oriented and they wanted to do it together. That is the power of simplifying goals and ensuring that everyone gets the same message. I didn't stop there, I committed to showing appreciation daily to each of my staff. If it wasn't a conversation to appreciate, it was a conversation on what needs to happen for that associate to take action. I am just as accountable for that lack of action and the next action from everyone on my team.

The reason why this is so critical is that ensures growth in your leadership journey and it shows your team that every action is to be discussed in appreciation or constructive feedback. Stopping at goal setting and waiting for the results to just come to you and your team is a recipe for failure and the same mistakes will happen. Skip the goal setting instead if you are not going to go all the way. I wouldn't suggest you skip it, but if you are not planning on evolving and levelling up from goal setting, your leadership growth will happen very slowly, if it even grows at all. I witnessed other leaders go from goal setting to getting the results targeted and even more, and this inspired me to do that and even more with myself and my team. On the other hand, I witnessed leaders that set goals and just stopped there, and this motivated me to not take that route. Waiting for results to just happen with no consistent action of giving feedback and evaluation and reflecting is not exactly leading and impacting lives in my opinion.

When you start to see the growth just happen, it will motivate you and your team to do more, and this is when you have to activate your next up levelling. I started to have friendly competitions within my team. Keyword: "friendly." This means we compete and go out of our way to help the competition as well. I am very competitive, and I was a sore loser for a long time. I learned over time that it is okay to fall, fail and get back up and not repeat the same mistakes over and over. I said to another manager in 2014 that I would beat their store's sales within the year of my new store being open. I did not even have a plan yet on how my team and I were going to do that, but I knew we would get it done. Sometimes, saying the goal out loud activates the action and provides a reason to endure the tough times while you're trying to get that result.

The day we crushed our store targets and beat the other store's targets, I made a call to say thank you to the other manager for the competition and for pulling along with all my smack talk. When I hung up the phone, it occurred to me that my team and I can do more in other areas. It did not stop there. We kept on pivoting forward. I strongly believe that leaders can take their team from point A to B by setting clear goals and not just stopping there but evolving in the process. Follow through with each goal and let that create endurance for the long term and future goals.

## BUILDING MOMENTUM

How did I create endurance for myself? I listened to self-growth podcasts that inspired me each month to contribute more to my leadership transformation, and this is something I shared and taught my team. I had some days that I would walk in and see no increase or impact made towards our results. It would be very easy to point the finger at someone or place the blame. Instead, I took the high road of asking questions and finding out what happened before concluding. I did not learn how to do this in one day. I saw the aftermath of jumping to conclusion without gathering facts. When I did that in the past, my team's morale was negatively affected, turnover of staff was high, and our bottom line suffered. I don't know about you, but I was more than excited to know what the alternative was. To lead my teams better, I had to observe other leaders in my leadership team and ask questions like "What would you do?" in different scenarios. My drive to seek knowledge never let me down in getting the answers and applying it to my work. You don't have to be perfect, but you can be persistent with your team in reaching your goals. I am a firm believer in that.

Another approach that I never take for granted is sharing what actions I am personally taking to reach my goals. It fires me up and shines a light on my path. It is a 'no point of return' feeling because there are goals to reach ahead. I would call up my direct report to share an action that my team and I have taken to get closer to reaching our goal. I would share with my late husband, Yusuff Bamigbade (RIP), the challenges I faced and what the outcome was. I am always excited when I am sharing. His excitement to hear my wins got me more excited and motivated to do more.

# Chapter 5

## Your Responsibility

Success brings on the responsibility to keep elevating and learning to be more effective than the last time you reflected on your journey. I heard this line quite frequently from some leaders that I crossed paths within my journey – "When I start doing this, they will expect it more." This is a problem that needs to be solved. As a leader, it is your responsibility to elevate and learn how to be more effective than your past actions. Yes, success brings on the responsibility to have more success. The challenge is to not stay stagnant. It is simple to keep doing what you have always done and keep getting the same results. I called this the comfort zone. There is a need for a stretch of the comfort zone. Imagine that if you and every other leader you know do everything in your power on your most productive day to stretch out of your comfort zones.

It will not only help us grow to our full potential, but also inspire the next generation of leaders to do the same. It is a recurring effect.

Fear of the responsibility of success is part of the reasons leaders don't do the required work in elevating their journey. I started working at McDonald's' at the age of 14. I always knew that I will help people and lead them in anything I do in my life. I realized this when I would walk home from school at age 9 with my cousins and younger brother and I would protect them by making sure we were all holding hands, not talking to strangers, and never letting go of each other's hands until we got home. I took responsibility for their safety and well-being without being asked to do so. They followed my lead because they believed in me and knew that I was doing it to get all of us home safe. I always felt so good and relieved when we made it home safe. The walk home happened when our school driver would forget to pick us up. Crazy, right? Instead of waiting there till dark, I took the initiative every time to start walking home. The point of my story is that trusting and working through the process of leading successfully is part of the solution to the fear of the responsibility of success.

In the first few months that I started working at McDonald's, I got promoted to a crew trainer. I got trained on how to train and I instantly fell in love with training as I saw my trainees growing and getting promoted as well. One of my managers said to me, "You should be a manager one day." It came to me as a shock, not because I couldn't do it but because I did not see anyone in management at the time that looked like me - black, young, and ambitious. I feared the responsibility of being the first of my kind to make it to management in that specific location. I thought about it over and over and believe me, it took me months to start believing that I could assume that role one day. All I needed to do was work hard and keep believing that it was possible. I feared that I will let down other black girls like me from pursuing the role if I failed to accomplish this. Over time, I used that as my motivation to do all that it took to make it to management and let my journey be the example of what to do or not to do. When I decided to let go of my fear of failure to succeed and focus on succeeding, I got promoted year after year and finally, into a restaurant manager role. I trusted the process despite its challenges along the way. My story inspired the next generation that would get their first job at McDonald's and I am content with this. Part of my purpose is to inspire and help others see opportunity and work with it to their advantage and impact change for the better of themselves.

## ALIGNING RESPONSIBILITY AND PURPOSE

I have the responsibility to live my purpose. It is to lead, inspire, and help others in my leadership journey. I have to show instead of expecting. Having a strong reason to motivate me is key to living my purpose. I feel empowered to speak up and be the symbol of evolving change. Imagine leading and allowing yourself to feel, breath, see and live through all that falls on your leadership path just so that you can fully live your purpose.

Sometimes we avoid conflict because of the following:

-   We are intimidated by our direct report

-   We are people pleasers

-   We hope that it won't come up again

-   We just don't like confrontations

-   We like complaining about problems instead of solving it

Avoiding conflict and not managing it is a problem in leadership, and until we do the work, it takes to know why we avoid it, we will remain in that place of avoidance and stagnancy. Another fact to this is that when you avoid conflict in your leadership, you start applying the same approach in your personal life. Another thing is, avoiding conflict management can be selfish. You are not the only one that doesn't grow. Your team and the ones that look up to you to lead stay stuck as well in building on that skill.

**Intimidated by Our Direct Report:** I avoided conflicts because I feared how my direct report would react or that I might lose my job. Both are very valid, and I was stuck with thoughts and feelings of not solving that conflict. Conflicts that are not managed or solved do not go away. It just sits in the back until it comes up again. I thought to myself one day, if my team was stuck with something like this within them and it is holding them back from growing, I would want them to talk to me about it to solve it. I had to put myself in my team's shoes and do as I would want them to do. I spoke to my direct report at the time about how I was being spoken to in front of my team and customers. I am always open to feedback, but I should receive it respectfully. I was sweating and shaking as I shared this with my direct report. What I did here was to activate the crucial step to managing conflict with my direct report. What happened next in my leadership journey with conflict management was just non-stop facing and working through each conflict and feeling empowered to always speak up.

As a result of this first crucial step and not stopping there, I now have empathy, psychological boundaries, and focus on the good when I am managing conflict with myself, clients, friends and family. There is so much power and growth in that for myself and the person I am interacting with.

**We Are People Pleasers:** Pleasing my direct team and my top leadership team took priority over talking about the uncomfortable things and important/tough conversations. Why bring up a conflict that needs to be managed and solved when everyone is happy with your performance and the results you are producing with your team? The thing is, I was holding everyone back from growing by pleasing them. I was enabling the lack of growth in working together to manage different conflicts. I clearly remember saying yes to requests or projects that were an inconvenience for me. It usually meant that I had to work more hours in addition to my 40+ hour week, and this also resulted in me being tired during the project timeline. You can say the people-pleasing act results in an I-can-do-it-all attitude. This did not work for me for a long time. I started to feel a drop in my energy and that was not a good thing for me because my energy is one of my most valued traits and this feeds fuel into other areas of my life.

This was my sign to stop people-pleasing. The only option was to start focusing on conflict management in this area. I started with my team – I started with declining someone's request for a busy day off or a schedule change. In the past, I would work to cover the operations when a manager on my team needed a last-minute favor. I did not stop there as this activated my planning skills. I had to plan six months in advance to accommodate last minute requests. When you already have a plan, it is more clear to say yes or no.

When I started saying no to projects that meant I would have to work more than I was working, I built psychological boundaries with my top leadership team. By not saying yes to everything, I was saying that my self-care is important and that I trust other leaders on my team to take on a project. Now, I plan well, and I don't feel guilty when I say no or feel pressured to say yes as a result of managing through the people-pleasing conflict.

## DON'T WAIT, TAKE ACTION NOW

**We Hope That It Won't Come Up Again**: Hoping and hope coming true are two different things. There is no action in hope, it is just a feeling and thought. Hoping for a conflict to just go away is quite gutsy in leadership. Solving it as it comes up is a required skill. I experienced a leader do this exceptionally well, and they made it look flawless. I saw the benefits and I picked up on some of the actions that I can build on to deal with conflict now and not wait for it to come up again. I experienced that when you avoid conflict, it will come up in a different form and even more complicated than before. And when constantly avoided, it could affect business results. For example, when a high performing employee shows up late regularly and receives no disciplinary action, but a low performer does the same and receives disciplinary action, this is an act of picking and choosing what conflict to solve. This behavior leads to low employee morale and high turnover. I choose to be consistent with managing conflict and not choose when and what I solve in the moment. As a result of improving and becoming an expert at acting now versus hoping in conflict resolution, I can coach my clients through each scenario of conflict and take each client through a specific process that can apply to different areas of their leadership.

## VIEWING CONFRONTATION AS AN OPPORTUNITY

**We Just Don't Like Confrontations:** This is a disease I suffered in elementary school. I am not talking about being rude to another person because they disagree with your opinion. Let's reword it as a respectful confrontation. An encounter that leads to a common solution for both parties. I dreaded ever disagreeing with a teacher or someone of authority. I did not want anyone to feel disrespected or call my parents to complain about something I had said or done.

What I did had never been done by any student before; I still do not know what came over me. Yes, I did apologize to my teacher after confirming that my actions were simply out of character for me. My parents, friends, and the rest of my family were very shocked by my behavior. Before I tell you the outcome of my actions, I will tell you what happened before I did the unspeakable. I believe that this is when my leadership journey was activated and my self-awareness began.

My teacher at the time was very passionate about her work, but she always intimidated every student. In my memory, her class was always a danger zone. At least, that's how I felt when I was in her class. She pushed us to our extreme potential to do well. We were not allowed to speak in that class. The discipline was out of this world, especially when any of us got something incorrect. Now I know that it happened for us to grow and be prepared for other challenges that we would inevitably encounter in the future. I did not look forward to school, and I couldn't wait to finish her class. I am grateful for what I learned from her, especially the skill to always push myself, even when I think that I am at my full potential.

The unfortunate happened when I got so sick that I missed a month or two off school. Part of me was worried about how much catching up I would have to do, but at the same time, I missed a month of my not so favorite class. That was the best part, and since my parents were so resourceful, they got my least favorite teacher to tutor me so that I can catch up. It was the worst that could have happened. I don't remember telling my parents about how I felt about her. I did something else instead to express what I was feeling. In an assignment, we had to use an adjective to describe a noun in a sentence. One of my sentences said, "--------------- is a wicked teacher." Why I chose that adjective when I knew my teacher would see it, I still can't tell. All I knew was that my frustration was overflowing, and I needed to put a stop to it. I got in trouble and you can imagine what happened. Throughout elementary school, I surprisingly had a great relationship with that same teacher. My sentence took our relationship to a positive one. When we don't confront a conflict respectfully, we are letting it build up. When there is no more room for it to be stored, it explodes in a form of anger. That is not okay, especially when you want to lead by example. My clients sleep better at night because they are empowered to manage conflict respectfully for the greater good.

## BE SOLUTION DRIVEN

A lot of us would rather complain about our problems than solve them: Some leaders enjoy talking about the problems, who should have done what and what should have been done. This would mean dwelling in the past for 100% of the time and missing the opportunities right in front of you. I can say that I did not experience this directly, but I did witness other leaders doing this. Giving power to what has already happened takes us back several steps behind the steps we have taken forward. This effect triples down to our team. What we do as leaders, our teams emulate. When it becomes a behavior, it would take more time to change it, especially when it is now part of the culture.

One of my mentors used to say to me, "Rasie, always go to the source when you have a problem." That is the best feedback that stayed with me for a long time. Conflicts are always going to happen, and our job as leaders is to manage it so that it doesn't escalate into a bigger issue than it already is. I learned how to respectfully manage conflicts with my direct report by coming up with the solutions before having that conversation. I think it is a waste of time to spend 100% of our energy and time examining the problem when we can forward think and solve the problem. I would not only come up with the solutions but draft a plan on how to execute them.

The problem and the solution should be looked at hand in hand to manage conflict effectively. Complaining did not get Obama to the presidency. He talked about the problems and how he will solve them to show that he was capable of being in office. Be clear about how you want to manage conflict; do it respectfully and with empathy, but if you are afraid of the responsibility of success, take one step towards that success and look back. That is you taking on the responsibility. Live your purpose as you should and show up as you would expect your team, family, business partners and community members to show up. Trust and work through the process.

# Chapter 6

## Use This to Measure Your Success

Talent and people development is a great measurement of a leader's success in any organization, business and community. The best part is that this measurement is free. You don't need a program to do any calculations or collect data. It is right in front of us. The time we spend on developing talent is not only a great reflection of what a leader knows but also a great motivator for high performing employees.

In 2010, I went through the highest turnover of staff that I could have ever imagined. I was working from dawn to dusk for weeks and when I wasn't at work, my phone still rang. The reality is, I was so focused on reaching the results that I dropped the ball in developing talent and continuously hiring for the future quarters. I remember calling other managers to ask for help with staffing and training. I was very embarrassed to do this; the embarrassing feeling is another topic to discuss of how I evolved from viewing the act of seeking help and support as embarrassing to seeing it as part of the process in my leadership journey. How could I have not seen this coming so I could prevent it? Those were the perfectionist thoughts in me and my ego taking a hit to the head. This was already going on for weeks and usually, it would take weeks until the new hires can work alone and be confident in meeting the expectations on each shift.

Even when all my new staff were hired and working, I was still working a lot of overtime and could barely catch my breath. My days went like this, wake up, drink coffee before getting to work, and eat my breakfast as quick as I could because I had no clue what I was walking into. I mentally prepared my mind and body for the worst. What a way to lead! All I knew for sure was that my team and I were going to bounce back and come back strong. I did not take this lesson and unfortunate situation in my business lightly. It was my responsibility to continue to develop talent in my team. It does not stop at me learning, but it sure starts with me.

There was already a development tree idea implemented by other managers. I needed to use this to continuously develop talent in my team and make more time to spend one-on-one time with each of my staff. The development tree is in pyramid style. Each manager is responsible for the development and mentoring of another employee, including the newest employee. This way, everyone is learning, and I had to do intense follow-up and encourage friendly competitions. Did I stop hiring? Nope, you guessed it right. Developing talent makes room for me to grow as a leader, and it also makes me more available for my team. As a result of this experience, I am very passionate about talent development. Because I have experienced the consequences of not developing talent, I choose to develop talent.

## MAKE TIME

Investing time and energy in developing talent in your team leads to genuine relationship building. Most leaders that are too busy to sit and have one-on-one conversation with their teams stay stuck because they are missing a genuine connection with every individual in their team. We can't buy time and energy. When it is gone, it is gone, and we can't go back in time to maximize the time and energy missed. I have a lot of energy that flows, and it keeps flowing when I am connecting with people. What did this mean to me in leadership? I can sustain and keep up my energy as I spend time and energy with my team on our goals. This translates to coming in fifteen minutes earlier or staying fifteen minutes later to do that extra. The extra can be having coffee with two people on my team per day to get to know them personally. Knowing what my team values and what is important to them can show me the need to do certain things differently. When I know that my associate, Suzie goes to church on Sundays, I will plan to make sure Suzie goes to church by scheduling her on another day or a different time of the day. These minor things don't cost the business any loss; it adds value by letting Suzie know that she is a valued employee. I did my one-on-one conversations for a short time, and it eventually became part of my routine.

My staff started to look forward to it, and it went on longer and stretched my creativity. I started having it during my working hours because of the value it was adding to the business. My team felt seen, heard and uplifted. Do this genuinely to get to know your team and see the passion and care you get from each person. It boosts morale, productivity and encourages people to want to genuinely be at work and do their best. My experience from the high turnover I had shared earlier was a motivating factor for me to do more than usual so I could develop talent and build genuine relationships with members of my team. One of my life goals is to impact everyone that I meet and help them see their full potential by sharing what I see and what they do well. I am a leader in all areas of my life, and it doesn't stop with my clients.

## LEADING AUTHENTICALLY IS NECESSARY

Showing up as you are is a very important responsibility. Why would you want to show up as anyone else? It might be because of what you see other leaders show everyone. But we might never know the true story. Showing up as you in your unique way is key. We need more leaders that show up and lead in their own way while they continuously evolve in their roles. It is very easy to see another leader lead differently and you wanting to do it the same way. Yes, be inspired, but don't be so focused on taking on every trait that you lose yourself in the process and lose focus on your leadership path.

One of my favorite quotes is, "Comparison is the thief of joy," from Theodore Roosevelt. These words resonated very strongly the first and many times I have heard them. When we spend our time and energy comparing our way of leading to other leaders, we miss many opportunities to "max out" as Ed Mylett would say. Imagine spending time and energy comparing and constantly thinking about it. That is not healthy. You are widening your focus to the wrong things; you are letting your team down when your business results could be more than you can imagine. I shared earlier in the last chapter about my friendly competition with another leader. The keyword there is 'friendly.' I encourage friendly competitions on my team but not comparison. When we lead authentically, we encourage leaders on our team to cultivate this necessary act in leadership.

Part of leading authentically is celebrating small wins. It took me a very long time to understand why celebrating small wins is so important. Do you get focused on the big goal that you lose focus of the small wins in the process? This is a problem in leadership. The solution isn't so simple, but it is attainable. These are the key reasons why you should celebrate small wins:

- To keep your team motivated

- To self-motivate

**To Keep Your Team Motivated** – Stopping to celebrate each person's and your team's win is bigger than we can imagine. Your team will feel heard, seen and happy. Put yourself in one of your staff's shoes and imagine working so hard and only getting a thank you or great job months later when the project is completed, or a goal is accomplished. That is painful, but unfortunately, some employees feel this way. It is time to solve this problem. Start small by looking for the small wins in one thing per day to two, then three and more from there. You don't stop at one. You continue elevating and evolving until it becomes routine and part of your authentic leadership style. Happy employees mean happy customers and then happy leaders. You have the choice and the time right now to make this change and celebrate the small wins.

**To Self-Motivate** – I mentioned that leading starts with us leading our lives. Leaders are more successful in leading their team, business, and community when they are experts at leading their own lives. Oprah said it best that when "we know better, we do better." Walking the talk privately and publicly in leadership is essential. It can be draining to keep going for that big win but imagine missing that shot when you have spent zero time celebrating your small wins. That would be a big hit emotionally, physically and mentally. You have no wins to show, and you missed that big win.

## LOOK FOR SMALL WINS

When I started to intentionally look for the small wins, a lot changed for myself and my past teams and now clients. Celebrating the small wins fed me energy, boosted my work esteem (it is a word now) and joy from within. I knew how I was doing, and it activated my self-reflections and those of my team as well. I was becoming more aware to how my strengths were working for me and what areas I had to work on to take my team and myself closer to our goals. Either you dance, buy yourself a gift, write it down, tell someone, it is necessary to celebrate your small wins. Go get your happiness from within and lead yourself and your team more authentically. The process of developing talent, leading authentically and building relationships should be fun in our community, business and with our teams.

We can measure our success from what we create with our people and how we lead. Measurements are always there and available for us, if we just seek them. Why seek feedback and use it as a way to measure our success and our results? Why do it when you can wait for your performance review of you and/or your business? Why should you do that when you can just look at the numbers? Why do it when your team is doing great right where they are?

It is time to break the cycle of waiting for someone else to do it first, or for your direct report to tell you to do so. I never understood the concept of waiting to be told to do something. If I know what to do and understand what needs to be done to impact change right now, I get it done. What I do for my clients and the results they get from working with me is the true measurement of my success. The awesome part is, I get to seek feedback throughout my Jumpstart process and reflect on the wins in the process.

## THE TIME IS NOW

It is time for every leader to break the cycle; help your business community and teams be successful and you become successful in the process. Talent and knowledge fuels empowerment. Think of yourself; if you did not know what to do in your leadership role, you will not feel confident to speak. Knowledge creates empowerment and confidence feeds empowerment. It is important and necessary for every one of my clients to feel empowered after working with me. I intentionally coach to deliver on this result. When we are empowered, we act solely to get those specific results.

In my previous experience in leadership at Starbucks, I would go home mentally tired because I was teaching and coaching on the spot and passing on my knowledge. I needed everyone on my team to know what I knew. Developing more leaders is key. The performance of everyone on my team was a great measurement of my success. The way each of my staff interacted with customers, support each other and deliver on our actions and goals showed me how I was doing in leading my team. Another result of these actions is that I gained credibility from my team and my customers. When you walk the talk in leadership, you not only help your team to do the same, but it brings you closer to those results because your team will help you get there. Why do it alone when you can do it with your team, business partners and community?

## Your Team Needs You

Your team needs you to teach and coach them in their development. Spend and invest your energy and time building healthy relationships and be reliable at all times. Your people are the number one reason why you are in your leadership role. As you evolve in your role and impact your team's talent, remember to celebrate the smallest wins; it matters. You will empower your team, break the cycle of waiting for measurements, and build your credibility in the process. This approach to measuring my success through talent and people development worked for me, and I continue this work with my clients. When you know it works, keep making it work for you by authentically leading yourself, team, business and community.

# Chapter 7

## Show Up Fully Present

Showing up each day with integrity and staying fully present says more about a great leader than the words said. We owe this to ourselves and others to show up just as we expect them to. Practicing and demonstrating the necessary things in leadership will result in consistency and high performance.

Sharing the necessary information frequently to stay transparent with your team and business partners is where we can start in leading with transparency. When no one is watching, that's when we know if integrity is our #1 value or #2. When you practice integrity as your number one value, you just have to show up as you. You don't need to worry about who's watching or who would be judging.

Especially when you're in a business and attracting a constant flow of customers in your path; you have to show up consistently to maintain those relationships and stay in business. When I say show up, I mean doing what you say you are going to do and being consistent with it. This tells your story, and you inspire others that look up to you, to show up in their truth.

In my business, I coach my clients in a private setting and before each call I have to prepare and deliver on the results I have committed to for each client. It is very important for me to share the necessary information in each session and offline to help my client fully transform to their most potential. How do I share necessary information frequently to stay transparent? Depending on what session and what topic that my client wants to improve on or develop on a specific skill, I intend to and always deliver all that I said that I will do to fast track their transformation. My clients' results are the #1 reason why I'm in business. It is my passion and my life's purpose to help each client and my audience grow and excel in their leadership journey. My clients pay for the speed as well. Leaders can do it on their own, but it might take years to get there. Working with me, leaders can reach their goals sooner and experience genuine happiness. There is always a way. Let's discuss the question – how do I share the necessary information to stay transparent with my clients? In my introductory call, I share how

I work with a potential client. I share what my framework is and what the results are. This is key in transformation. My clients need to be fully informed of where we are going when we take off. Being transparent with this information creates trust, a high level of commitment, excitement and a clear vision of the path being walked. Imagine you are driving somewhere, and you have no clue where you are going, and it is just fog in your way. You will be overwhelmed, nervous, scared, anxious and filled with all the uneasy feelings that come with the unknown. Some of my clients had experienced this before doing the work through my jumpstart process. It is my utmost responsibility to do the work in clearing that fog on my first call. Who doesn't want some certainty, right? The uncertain things will happen and most times, we have no control over it. Certainty of growth and results brings some ease to our nerves and we get excited even if we would have to move outside our comfort zone. Another reason why I must stay transparent is that my client is investing just as they would in business or necessities in their lives. When we invest, we want certainty and return of investment. Transparency is key from my posts on my social media platforms, direct messaging with my connections, zoom calls, in-person conversations, introductory calls and coaching calls. It starts from where I start and what is awesome as well, is that the clients that decide to work with me, already know me from my interviews, posts and videos. It is similar to going into an interview and you have read everything about the job you are applying for and you have connected with someone that has worked in that role. It kicks in some confidence and trust boost to show up and do what it takes to get to the other side of the job in this example.

## TRANSPARENCY IS KEY

I help my clients become more transparent with themselves first, then they can do this at a high frequency with their team, business, family and community. Creating a safe space for my clients to feel comfortable and share their deepest thoughts and feelings to transform their leadership journey is a necessity. Some leaders are very optimistic that they fail to be honest with what they are feeling. On the other hand, some leaders share too much on the problems they are experiencing and not support each problem with a solution. Sometimes, we have leaders that do both. Creating the space for the work to start happening with transparency with each of my clients uniquely is a must in my Jumpstart Process. I worked with a client that could not be transparent with their leader about the problems they were dealing with and they couldn't share that kind of information with their team. It is not your team's job to fix your deepest problems, nor is it your direct report. Now, my client was stuck in dealing with their problems. They did not trust their direct report to work through their deepest problems. They had the fear of being judged, being looked down on or losing credibility with top leadership. That was their deepest problem and as a result of working with me, my client was able to speak up, be transparent constructively and happier in their leadership journey.

When a leader models this behavior of transparency, they inspire and motivate their teams, business partners, and especially the ones that look up to them and count on them to lead the way. Transparency keeps people connected deeply, and it activates better communication in leadership. It starts with our leaders. Have you heard the saying, "Always do the right thing, especially when no one is watching?" My parents said this to me once when I was maybe seven years old, and it stuck with me to this day. I always told my staff in my previous leadership roles to do this and improve on it. Yes, there will be opportunities; when you see the opportunity, seize it and be better. What is doing the right thing? In my work, it means doing what is best for my clients at all times; seeking feedback so that I can improve and adding value to my Jumpstart Process. Nothing can be perfect, but we can strive for perfection. For example, during each of my coaching calls, I make sure my phone is on silent and not in immediate sight so that I don't get interrupted. Doing the right thing when no one is watching is also a demonstration of care. Being prepared before my calls show that I care about my clients, their results, time and energy. Doing the right things for your team and business means that you only have to walk one walk.

You might relate to this story: It was one of the biggest pet peeves in my leadership journey, and I still don't understand this up to this day. Maybe it wasn't meant to be understood. It was meant to be done because that is what it is, and no questions asked. You may take this personal if you are all for this in your organization. I am shining a light on this because it shows a lack of transparency and an inability to do the right thing. I am fired up as I share this. My passion to fully deliver on results is overwhelming in a great way.

## HERE IT GOES

When the top leadership team visits any location that I would be leading, the preparation goes like this; There is a plan for that day. There is a plan for the day before. There is no plan for the day after. We go back to normal. What!? Yes! We had to make sure it all goes perfectly even if our team was stressed, nervous and on edge and that includes me. I would have some crazy dreams of everything going wrong. That is the fear of not showing up perfectly with my team to impress our top leadership team. I had amazing female leaders in my journey that wanted to see what was happening and not what is great because they were visiting. I have so much respect for their approach, and it inspired me to challenge that concept and do better in my role. This is where the gap is, and I empathize with this. What about the customers? They deserve and need this level of care and attention to detail during each of their visits. When there are no clients and customers, we won't have a job to go to or people to serve and make an impact for the greater good. This is how I saw it, and it motivated me to consistently talk about it with everyone on my team.

Another example at home and we all do this or have done it at some point; we tidy up for our visitors. What if you did this for yourself once a week and enjoy that treat? Start internally and go from there. Leave it to your customers and clients to say how awesome your business is. You are in business because of who buys from you, and that should be your priority. Be transparent and do the right thing.

Would you say that you are fair to everyone you work with? Do you treat everyone equally? This applies to your team and customers. It is human nature from what I have observed and experienced that when we don't feel treated fairly, it affects our health negatively. I love this saying that I have heard Oprah say many times – "that people will always remember how you make them feel." The best way to fully improve our level of fairness is by putting ourselves in others' shoes. I saw this from time to time - some managers would speak to a high performer with respect and the low performer in a demeaning tone or the other way around. It breaks my heart every time. Whether they are high performers or low performers, customers, clients, and employees are humans and should be treated fairly and with respect. Are you stuck and not sure why people are reacting a certain way to your words, directions and expectations? You want your team and business to grow, but you are just stuck in the same place. I challenge you to put yourself in your clients' shoes, in your team's shoes, and be objective about what you feel and hear. This will elevate your effectiveness in leading. Transparency, doing the right thing for the ones you work with or work for and being fair works and the results are well worth it. An increase in employee productivity, increase in customer retention and a booming bottom line are just some of the most incredible results you can enjoy from taking action now.

# Chapter 8

## Many Count On You to Lead the Way

Taking care of ourselves is being respectful to ourselves, the people we interact with, and the ones that look up to us; we have a responsibility to show up as the role model in our leadership journey. Whether you are leading consciously or subconsciously, people will do what you do. Someone is watching what you are doing, copying your behaviors, and acting similarly. The responsibility that comes with leading should not be taken lightly and should be handled with tenderness, care, and loving. Where do we start to self-care? From my experience, three things are crucial. I struggled with these three things for a long time, not knowing what to say or do for better self-leadership.

Those three things are lack of self-care, self-doubts, and lack of reflection.

**SELF-CARE**

I remember feeling overwhelmed and just exhausted on most days. The feeling won't go away. Sometimes, it would hit right before I start my day at midday or when I got home. My head would feel full, heavy, and restricted; it felt as if I was not supposed to move it to the right, left, up, or down. My eyes would feel heavy, as if I had not slept for a few days. I would always feel hungry and eating very quickly, relieved a bit of stress. I stopped a few times to say to myself, "This will pass in due time." It was a lie; the feeling of being overwhelmed comes and goes, but that doesn't mean you have solved it. If you are feeling overwhelmed, you are not alone. All leaders experience this once or more, depending on their current problems. Not practicing self-care can increase how overwhelmed we feel. This is how I felt when I wasn't practicing self-care by doing the three important actions. When I started to express and take action on these three important actions, I started to feel the shift, the transformation, the weight leaving my body, and my mind making room for other important things.

The first thing I started to do (and it took everything in my body to do this) was something we struggle with when we are new to leadership or are in a new role in our organization. We try to build our credibility and show that we can lead and get results. Asking for help is the first thing I learned to do to avoid feeling overwhelmed all the time. I am talking about the kind of help you seek when you can do it yourself at a higher level. The kind of help that you seek to protect your time and energy for the more important tasks. Saving your energy and time for the tasks that will increase your bottom line and get you the results. It is okay to ask for help. Some forms of asking for help are delegating, building a team that can rely on each other, creating time to let your team know how they are doing, and letting your team know what support you need from them. In my first leadership role, I was the only black, young, female in my team. I always had to work harder, show up earlier than others, and be mindful of how I was showing up. What people in my organization perceived mattered. I needed to show up for all black young females. I still take that very seriously today. I always said yes, even when I wanted to say no. I read this somewhere and I am unsure of the source, but it said, "it is okay to ask for help." I started with my peers; I started to pick their brains and ask questions like, "how would you do this?" With this approach, I created meaningful relationships and allies along the way.

As I learned from my peers, I started to do the same with my team and rely on their strengths throughout my leadership journey in the food and beverage industry. I shifted more time from doing it all to delegating, following up, and giving constructive feedback. The feeling of being overwhelmed would come from time to time, but I knew that asking for help would help me be more effective. The results from asking for help and doing it consistently were an increase in happiness for me from within, better relationships with my peers and team, an increase in our bottom line, and higher productivity.

## TRUSTING SELF

When you are asking for help, you need to know that what you are doing is necessary and you can gain more by working with your team. This brings us to the 2nd thing I now cherish and continue to build on. I needed to have self-trust in all the decisions I made. The doubts, fears, and worries can offset self-trust. When I am overwhelmed, I start to doubt myself by measuring where I was in that moment based on the problems I was facing and the results I was not achieving. This thought process is real, and it can take us by surprise. Those moments when you feel exhausted, and it feels like the world is against you and you can't catch a breath can be a very dark place. It happens, but thankfully, there is a solution to it. It is harder to do but with the right coach, mentor, or teacher, you can transform this experience to become part of your leadership journey. Why did I not trust myself? I was not clear on my vision. My WHY always added fuel to the fire in me, and my lack of self-trust added a fire extinguisher to my fire. Imagine that back and forth. Self-trust would bring me self-satisfaction, self-love, and boost my self-esteem. I started to have more constructive self-talk. I spoke to myself as if I was speaking to my late husband in his lowest moments (RIP Yusuff Bamigbade). I started to practice self-compassion even to this day. I started to understand that I was only in control of my actions. Self-trust is the next action to build on. Knowing my values, strengths, and what results I delivered is necessary for trusting myself. When I coach each of my clients on a call, I confidently take them through my Jumpstart Process. I am not overwhelmed because I am prepared. I know that I have the skills to deliver on the results discussed, and I remind myself of my accomplishments by celebrating my wins consistently. This is a result of self-trust. Imagine your team helping you and you trusting every decision you make. The overwhelming feeling has no place to exist.

## ENGAGING IN SELF-REFLECTION

The last thing is one of my favorites; different leaders do this differently. It is a significant way to map things out and be able to see them clearly. You can take another step and post it in your home or office so that it can be a reminder in the moment of doubts, worries, and fears. I made time to reflect on where I was going, where I was at, and where I was now. When I feel overwhelmed, I would read this over and over to ground myself and come back to the present. When we are overwhelmed, we think of the past and future mostly. We think of what could or could not happen on repeat. Read that last sentence a couple more times. It makes you not want to be in that state and take action now. How do I reflect? I use different journals; I have my personal, business, and clients' journal to write down my wins, results, and aha! moments. In my personal diary, I journal how my emotional intelligence has been transformed, what values I have added to my self-growth, and what I am feeling as a result of my self-growth. In my business journal, I take note of who I have impacted by writing down peoples' comments, resonating words from messages, and how many posts I have put out to motivate people and to activate the need for leaders to take that big step to transform in their leadership journey. In my clients' journal, I write down what my clients' have messaged me in the moment of appreciation for my coaching. Doing this reflection consistently gives me room to remind myself of my wins. Reflecting is key and making time for it is necessary to continue our work in leading effectively.

Start asking for help, trusting yourself, and making time to reflect on your work. This is how to work through that overwhelming feeling. You can hire a coach to hold you accountable for doing this and at maximum speed. I also discovered that my interactions became more intentional and purposeful. This is because by doing the things that are necessary to keep role modeling for my clients, my community, and my family, I was also taking care of myself. You can make a goal to practice self-care. You can start working towards this goal. What about when things get tough? How do you keep going? Everyone needs a coach to keep the momentum going and for a higher level of accountability. I know that no matter what the challenge is in my entrepreneurial journey, I can reach out to my coach, be honest with what is going on within me, and get honest guidance and support.

The reality about our leadership journey is that anything can happen, personally and professionally, and it can significantly affect our day-to-day leadership tasks and presence. I have been on the other side of not practicing self-care by refusing to ask for help, trusting myself less, and spending less time reflecting and, as a result, feeling very overwhelmed. Some days, you can feel as if it is permanent. But it only becomes permanent when we don't take action to transform this behavior into our leadership journey. It starts with you and going forward, others that you already inspire will do it as well. This is more effective leadership that starts with you and goes on for generations. It is a beautiful responsibility to lead ourselves and others because in so doing, we are changing lives and impacting change for the greater good.

# Chapter 9

## Believing Starts with You

Keep believing in yourself because when you do, you inspire others to do the same. Read that one more time and feel every word. When we say we believe in ourselves, what does that mean? Do we believe what we say to others, especially our teams, family and friends? These are questions I started to ask myself when my team and I were stuck producing consistent results and not improving. Sometimes, we say what our goals are, but the question is, do we really believe that it is achievable? Do we start to believe in ourselves when *we surprisingly* accomplish our goals?

When I was in primary (elementary) school, I excelled academically, and this made my parents very proud. I didn't necessarily believe in myself and I will tell you why. I was very focused on impressing my parents that I would study hard even during lunch breaks just to be number one in my class or come in 2nd. My dad knew and still knows what my potential is and he genuinely believes that I can do anything I set my mind to. He did not sign my report card when I came 2nd place in class. I know he did that to push me to my fullest potential and guess what; it worked. To be honest, disappointing my parents is the last thing I wanted, and it is something I wouldn't be able to live with. Fear of the consequence builds up my momentum to start believing in myself and continue working hard to get that 1st place in class. I would even blame it on my classmate for having 1st place, when I would come in 2nd in my class. I laugh at this now as I still remember the names of those classmates that would kick my butt off the 1st place from time to time. If my Dad did not believe that I could, it would have taken me longer to grasp this concept and do the work that it takes to keep believing. This is what it takes at times, the support from our biggest cheerleaders to give us that extra push. Who is your biggest cheerleader? This is important to know because we all need at least one person that will support us with love and constructive feedback.

## HOW DO I KEEP BELIEVING WHEN CHALLENGES AND TRAUMAS HAPPEN?

One guaranteed part of the process is that it gets harder to keep believing. When I moved to Canada, I was overwhelmed with gratitude for the opportunity. The opportunity to learn, grow and be anything I wanted to be. The resources were overflowing and what blew my mind was that I didn't have to pay for extra help in understanding a topic after school hours. This wasn't for free back home. I appreciated that so much.

The first time I had to question myself academically was when I had to take an English and Math test. The school administration needed to know if I was qualified to be in Grade 9 because I started school a year earlier than my age group and the principal was shocked. I can still remember how I felt when I was told that I would have to repeat a grade because of my age. Mind-blowing, right? I did not pay attention to this, but I was stereotyped and put into a category. I was a black child from Africa and a grade ahead of my age. I couldn't be smart enough to start in a grade ahead of my age group. On this day, I was hurt, and I questioned what I had believed in for a long time. I assumed that I was not smart enough to be in Grade 9 and I would get to that level of intelligence at some point. The one thing that this experience did was introduce me to another level of hard work, the kind of hard work where you do not expect anything to be handed to you; you work hard to be a better version of yourself. My self-esteem was crushed at age 13 and I am still healing. As I write this, the tears are beginning to form in my eyes, but we must always remember that some unfortunate things will happen that would make us question our self-belief. One event can do this, pointing us to the fact that there is a lot of work to be done. Especially when you are told that you are not good enough by someone that doesn't even know you at all.

## DID I START BELIEVING IN MY SELF AGAIN?

Absolutely and making it to honor roll did add fuel to the flames of my self-belief. When people doubt you, you don't have to take the doubt. You can leave it where they dropped it and walk away or just refuse to pick it up. I have done this for myself, and because of my experience and not giving up on myself, I can successfully help each of my clients to evolve in their self-leadership. To lead your life better, you have to believe in yourself and this requires work. The distractions are real, and they are out there to challenge us. It is part of the process and it doesn't go away. It just changes in form. The gift of my experience is that I did not have to do it alone; I had support in some shape or form. My WHY was the big driver in staying highly motivated to see that I graduate from high school with impressive grades and do more from there. Keep believing in yourself.

Other factors also keep us from believing in ourselves. Whether we are aware of it or not, it is there and it brings on self-doubt, worries and fears. When we lack this factor, it can make it very difficult to lead. The term "fake it till you make it" will not save your leadership reputation. It is our responsibility to keep learning, teaching and inspiring to fuel this factor. Who wants to walk in the dark and have no clue what they are doing in the dark in the first place? That is what happens when you lack self-confidence in your leadership role. When you lead with confidence and belief in yourself, leading gets more enjoyable.

When I started working at Starbucks, I remember it being very busy during the times I was being trained. It was during Frappuccino happy hour (if you are a Starbucks customer, you know all about this). It is half off Frappuccino at the time. It was very busy, and I had to make one drink after the other for a full eight-hour shift and I did all the mistakes you can imagine. This is what I learned about this experience. I was hired as an operations manager, and this eight-hour experience was a blessing. Not only did I become an expert at making these drinks, but I did it with my team. They trained me and they built trust in me after I made all the mistakes and got better. The keyword here is 'built.' I am sure it was broken in the first hour before it was built in the eighth hour. After I completed my training, I worked in a different position every week to build on my confidence. I built credibility with my team as well and strong relationships.

When I worked with a different company, I grew tremendously out of my comfort zone and I was challenged to adapt to a different environment. Over time, I built the confidence of knowing that leading is my passion and I am great at it. It takes confidence and clarity in my passion and purpose to say this. Another thing that worked for me was that I didn't do things because everyone was doing them. I was always inspired to create and face the most challenging things. You can say that growth and staying out of my comfort zone feeds my energy. I think it is easy to follow the crowd and harder to be the lone wolf. If being the lone wolf brings me growth and helps me help my clients in the process, that sounds like a blast to me. When you say, 'I am leading this project, team, family or community,' it comes with the responsibility to believe in yourself and inspire others to do the same. Leadership starts with you; someone is watching what you are doing and mirroring the exact behavior.

# Chapter 10

## Claim Your Gift

Our Our emotions can be a gift or detrimental to our success. Continuous learning of our emotional intelligence is a necessary factor in our growth and influence of others. It depends on how you see your emotions. It always starts with the awareness of where you are with your emotional intelligence. The awareness can change your course of leading others for the greater good. I learned this in my own way, and I wasn't taught. I did not know it was called emotional intelligence until I heard leaders using this term. There is so much power in emotional intelligence when you do the work to improve it for the benefit of yourself-leadership and leading others. It starts with you.

Something significant shifted my emotional intelligence. I thought I was strong at this skill until I faced challenges that made it not so easy. I am talking about challenges where you can feel the heaviness run through your body and you just want the weight to be lifted off. That kind of challenge doesn't just go away, you can suppress it and push it down, but it sure comes back up in a different form and most times worse than before. What does emotional intelligence mean? To me, it means that I need to be emotionally aware of what is happening with my mind, body and soul. I need to stay connected and feed my intelligence the right things to keep growing in managing and expressing my emotions.

When a baby cries, it means that they need something and for them to stop crying, they need that particular thing immediately. As we grow, we come to understand that crying is not going to get us what we want. Some people will complain, take out what they are feeling on others, scream to express their emotions or just stay quiet and let it build up. But is that a healthy way to lead our lives? Every leader's journey is unique and all these ways and methods of expressions I have mentioned work for some and not for others. Let me share what I learned from leaders in my journey, including my teachers, mentors, and coaches.

When I worked with a leader that always complained and shared everything they were frustrated about, I felt very awkward. I thought, "why do I need to know this and what is the value here?" Then, I was so confused about why they got so frustrated as they kept mentioning that one thing I missed and dropped the ball on. It hurt each time, and I would remind myself not to express myself in that manner when leading my team. I needed to do better than that. The thing is sharing and seeking empathy works for some leaders. What happens though is that high performers who want to grow with that organization or company are pushed farther away. Also, when a leader puts their team on the receiving end of hearing what they are frustrated about, who is there for each person on that team when they need to share their frustrations? This is why this method didn't work for me. It was important for me to be on the receiving end for my team and find another source to air out my frustrations.

## WE ARE ALL HUMANS AND VENTING IS A NECESSITY

Whether it is one person, your journal or just in your thoughts, we need to express what we are feeling constructively, so that we can arrive at a solution for that specific issue and grow through the process. Clients I have worked with struggle to keep their emotions neutral in uncertain situations and while dealing with conflict. This is where it gets hard. You can learn all about emotional intelligence and understand it but if you don't work through each situation with what you have learned, there is no growth and lack of results. If you are at this stage of expressing your emotions, know that you are not alone as many leaders experience this. What you do about what you know is what matters. It is never too late.

When I worked at McDonald's, there was a sentence that I would always say to my new hires from the employee handbook - it was along the lines of being present and leaving our problems at the door when we walk into work. I firmly believed that until I started to do the same with my personal struggles when I would go home. When you start to build a habit, it is tough for our minds to differentiate the environments and block out what needs to be blocked. Boundaries are necessary and in time, I realized that it is okay for my team to share what challenges they were faced with outside of work. This is specifically important in an environment where most teams spend most of their life with their coworkers and less time at home. It is necessary for team members that are living in an uncomfortable environment at home to find their haven at work. Every leader needs to create this space for their teams, business partners, family and community members. Yes, make boundaries and foster a healthy working environment.

When I decided to stop allowing my emotions to dictate how and when I was coaching, training, teaching or mentoring, I knew it was going to be a tough and necessary transformation. What inspired me to do this differently was a comment my assistant manager said to me when I was seeking feedback. These words resonated, and I felt very accountable and had to start showing up differently and consistently. The words were, "I don't know what mood you will be in on most days and this makes me nervous to approach you and ask questions." I felt responsible for my assistant manager to feel this way. We all have bad days but being emotionally intelligent means showing up for my team regardless of how I was feeling that day and not showing up as unapproachable. It was tough to do this. I had a lot of pain and struggles I was personally experiencing at the time, and this was a wake-up call. A wake-up call that my emotions were getting the most of me and that is not how I wanted to lead.

I can say that I am emotionally intelligent until the next opportunity to grow in this area comes up. When these emotions come up from what someone did, what result you didn't get, or who hurt your feelings, it is important to stop and witness that emotion. Be compassionate and don't judge it. It is trying to tell us something. I learned that it was something that I needed to feel and heal to lead my life and others more effectively. This experience of being curious and practicing self-compassion has helped me build on my emotional intelligence. Another thing that tends to hold leaders back from being more intelligent with their emotions is the comfort zone.

When I was showing up in different moods and my team was unsure of when to talk to me, that is the comfort zone. I was leading this way because I was comfortable doing this and oblivious to how my team felt. My curiosity led me to improve this way of leading. I can't even imagine being that leader and I am always grateful for the leader I am becoming and for the feedback I receive from my teams in the past and now, from my clients. Don't be content with the comfort zone. Get curious when emotions arise in different situations. Choose to lead more effectively by investing time and energy in your emotional intelligence.

# Chapter 11

## Avoid It or Deal with It

Learning how to manage conflict objectively is key when you are climbing the corporate ladder because one wrong move can be detrimental to your growth in the workplace. I experienced this quite a few times in my leadership journey. I wish someone had told me that if you say the truth when top leadership asks what help you need; it will be interpreted as asking for too much. That is how I felt when what I said was dismissed without any follow-up or feedback. At some point, I thought to myself, 'Should I stop coming up with solutions?' 'Should I just do it and not say it out loud? Or 'should I just not speak so much in meetings?' These are questions that ran through my mind. I am a thinker; I think a few steps ahead before I make a step, and this has been one of my greatest strengths in my leadership journey. I don't like being rushed; I value peoples' time as much as mine. This motivates me to always be prepared to deliver more than what is expected. I would plan on what I needed help with before meetings with my direct reports or leadership team. Imagine getting super prepared, only to get shut down by the body language in a room and then dismissed with no feedback or follow-up on what I shared. Guess what? This pushed me to find out what my opportunities were and to improve and excel at them. I get excited to work on my weaknesses and add value to my leadership role.

Climbing the ladder can be easier for others and difficult for some. Whether you are working hard or not, some other factors would be considered before you get that promotion. I am very fond of growth; climbing the ladder is something that fueled my energy to keep giving 200%. Wherever you are in your leadership journey, do not stop working hard when you don't get that promotion. You don't know whose life you are changing by being consistent. Someone is always watching and doing exactly what you are doing or close to it. Beware, leaders; people want to be where you are at and do the things you are doing.

I am about to share with you how I managed conflict and moved from being too nervous to speak up, to speaking up constructively and respectfully and being unapologetic about what I said. Most of my clients were stuck at refusing to deal with conflict and being frustrated about it. This started to affect their personal lives and motivated them to hire me. The overwhelming feeling and being frustrated about how you're saying the things you say are real. When you let things stay down, unexpressed, suppressed, said to the wrong party or venting at home, other problems can be created like anxiety, panic attacks, loss of trust, taking work home and mood swings. I did that, and it only put my health at risk; I learned this the hard way, and that is why I solve this problem for my clients. Because of my experience dealing with different conflicts with myself, my previous team, customers and my clients, I am passionate and eager to help others through them. Conflict management is key to leading your life and that of others. It is one thing that most leaders avoid and the most necessary factor in continuing to build relationships. I learned that resolved conflict between two people makes the relationship stronger and when things are gone unsaid, it creates a lack of trust.

Not speaking up was tough for me when I experienced working with a leader that micromanaged. I did not understand this concept, and the struggle was real for me. Nothing was good enough, and perfection was the only way. It was exhausting. I felt like I was working all the time, processing what my direct reports reaction would be on our next visit. I want to make something clear - this approach worked until it didn't work anymore, and I am grateful for this experience. Not only did I work through this for myself, but I also help my clients through this because of my experience. It is an understatement to say that I am grateful to my leader at the time for this experience. I am glad I made it through and I'm strong and able to tell you this story.

There were certain things that I didn't say because I was very intimidated and nervous that I would be mistaken for not wanting to do the work. I cared about the perception of others, so I didn't speak up about how I was feeling. I reassured myself that I was a strong woman, and I could handle anything no matter how hard it was. This is what I said to myself until I couldn't take it. What happened next? I started to have anxiety attacks and then panic attacks in the middle of the night. I started to not feel valued, put down and spoken to differently compared to my peers. I felt hurt, unseen and not acknowledged. It was a very difficult time. I felt unmotivated to come into work, but I showed up each day for my team. I dreaded seeing my leader. I felt sick to my stomach because I did not know how long I could take it. Was I going to lose my job if I spoke up? There are qualified and more qualified people that could do my job. Now, I am not only anxious but also fearing that I might lose my job. A visit to the doctor because of my random anxiety attack at work and in front of my team gave me the wake-up call I didn't think I needed. I was embarrassed, and I knew that I needed to speak up immediately, in a respectful, fact-only way. I did not want to take pills to help me calm down or help me sleep. I am very sensitive to medication and would have to be in excruciating pain to even take a Tylenol. I decided it was time to have that conversation. I was sweating in the minutes leading to my conversation with my direct report while I read over what I had written down. I was ready to put my health first, to be treated fairly, feel valued, heard, seen and given a chance to make mistakes and learn from them. I sat down, said everything word-for-word as I practiced. I was nervous, but I remembered that the reason why I was having that conversation was more important than my nerves. I felt this sudden relief after I spoke. Spoiler alert! Nothing changed after this conversation with my direct report. If anything, I attracted more attention to myself and started to feel the unfairness in meetings. You know what though? I spoke up, and I was so proud of myself. I made a promise to myself to continue to speak up respectfully and constructively, no matter how tough the conversation. I am only in control of my actions. Always let your values guide you and treat people with kindness no matter what.

This was the first of many difficult conflicts I would be faced with. My first experience prepared me to always speak up during the next years in my leadership journey. Trust how you are feeling and reward that conflicted feeling with a solution. Know what your strengths are and add value to them so that you can inspire others to do the same. As my business coach, Fabienne would say, "double down on your strengths first and focus on that." Hire someone else to complement your weaknesses. I dare you to lead in your own way and inspire others to do the same, regardless of the fear of climbing that ladder or feeling intimidated by top leadership.

# Chapter 12

---

## Would You Like to Lead in Your Truth?

You might already have a coach or are still looking for one. I think that everyone needs a coach in their life. Whether it is to lead your life more effectively, help your team reach their results sooner or just excel in a specific area of your life, a coach helps you get there faster, in a structured manner, and get the results you have longed for.

I have shared with you the steps I took in my leadership journey, which I now implement into my framework for each of my clients. I have shared how these steps impacted my journey. I feel very empowered, and I am a firm believer in sharing with others what worked for me.

This can be a starting point for you to apply more effectiveness to your leadership journey. Whether you hire a coach, are thinking about hiring one or having an accountability partner, you can start from here.

## 8 Steps to Becoming Your Most Authentic Self in Your Leadership Journey

1. Get clear on your goals. Visualize the feeling of being at your desired destination of results and transformation.

2. When you are decided that you are a leader or if someone looks up to you (which means you are leading), you are responsible for adding value continuously to your role. Are you going at your full potential speed? This is a question to ask yourself when reflecting on your work.

3. One of the most effective ways to measure your success is by evaluating how your team is growing. Are you investing time in their talent development and people skills?

4. Showing up to be present, do the right thing for those you lead and doing what you said you will do makes a significant impact on your leadership journey.

5. Role modeling self-care and setting clear boundaries shows your team how to prioritize self-care, care for others and have

healthy interactions. There is a big gap in this area of leadership.

6. Self-belief starts with you. If you do not believe it, it won't happen. It is that simple. It starts with you; lead the way and do what it takes to take people where they need to go and be.

7. Build on your emotional intelligence at home and work. It can be a gift or be detrimental to your progress. You can lead more authentically when you put in the work to grow your EQ.

8. Conflict management not only helps with your interaction with your team or direct report, it can help you at home also. I focus on the objectivity of the conflict with each of my clients. We all struggle with self-conflict similar to the conflict with others.

These steps can guide you in deciding what and how you can take that next step that would help you lead your teams more effectively. It starts with you getting unstuck from where you are and refusing to make the same mistakes and not get the results you truly deserve.

Hire a coach, work with a mentor, or have an accountability partner to increase your speed in reaching the results that you long for. You don't have to do it alone. You can get there sooner and enjoy the process of getting there. Speed and fun are necessary for your leadership journey.

# Chapter 13

**◆•————————•————————•◆**

# Become The Authentic Leader You Are Meant to Be

## WHY I WROTE THIS BOOK

I wrote this book to inspire leaders to do what it takes to keep evolving in their leadership role. There isn't one path to leading teams, businesses, communities and ourselves. Owning our authenticity will make room for the fullest potential of our growth to happen. Our people are a key component of evolving, especially when we continue to set the example by being authentic. Not only is it necessary to learn and grow in our leadership journey, we should also not become complacent and comfortable. My passion for growth in leadership gets fired up when I see leaders get comfortable in their role and accepting "This is the way we have always done things." I think it is an unproductive way to lead. There is no such thing. We have the responsibility to keep growing and learning. By doing this, we are inspiring the next generations of leaders to learn from us and do better in their leadership journey. One of my favorite Oprah quotes, "When we know better, we do better," explains itself. We will make mistakes, but what matters is what we do after the fact. This is the definition of an evolving leader.

The success of our business relationships, community improvement and self-development speaks volumes about how you're doing as a leader. When our people are growing, this means that we are doing something right. Some leaders I have worked with become intimidated and passive-aggressive with high performers on their team. I perceived it as they were not comfortable with someone on their team being strong in areas that they had weaknesses in. The awesome opportunity here that most leaders miss is that we are not going to be experts at everything we do, and this is okay. That's why we have the advantage and capability to hire someone that excels at that and learn from them. Leadership involves working well with your team. Knowing yourself and what you excel at is a key component to succeeding in leadership. If I don't know what I am good at or what areas I need to improve in, I would be leading blindly. This not only affects us, but it also affects our team, business and community. Imagine leading the people that you care about into a war zone. If you just take a moment and be clear about your vision, you can lead everyone the right way and help yourself and your team grow throughout the process.

Another reason why I wrote this book is to shed some light on self-care for leaders. Our passion and lack of trust in our team can push us to the least extreme of self-care. It doesn't mean that sleeping better, taking breaks, disconnecting after and before work reduces the value of your organization. What it does is impact your health positively and encourage your team to do the same. When I worked 55 hours a week, I was not inspiring my managers and supervisors to be in my role. The ones I did inspire had already decided that the next role had to happen and inspired or not, they were highly motivated to get there. We miss the gap of inspiring potential leaders because they don't see qualities that they aspire to build on. They will see the qualities, but self-care neglect can push them away from pursuing roles in leadership. Research has proven time over time that employee productivity and engagement increases as a result of self-care in companies. How awesome is that?

Leading is not just about leaders being the one that makes the decision, it is about the team.

Involving your team in decision making and making them part of the problem-solving shows that you value your team and that you are a team leader. When I maxed on asking experts on my team for their input and bringing that solution and process to action, I gained not only their trust but loyalty. I trusted and received that trust back. It wasn't what I was aiming for but that is the result of valuing members on your team. People who feel valued will always do what it takes without being asked and they will highly perform especially when you hold everyone accountable to the same standard.

Leaders should not seek gratification and validation outside of themselves. When you don't receive it when you expect it, this can sink your self-motivation. I heard leaders say, "I didn't even receive a thank you after all that work." When you are content that you have done all that it took to the best of your ability, that is all that matters. Be happy that you are capable of so much more and you are getting results and ask your team for feedback continuously.

## MY TAKE-HOME MESSAGE TO THOSE IN LEADERSHIP

Lead in your authentic way and inspire those you lead to do the same. If you have decided to lead in your truth and you're ready to do the work, I have a freebie for you. Claim your freebie @ www.rbjumpstartcoaching.com/ebookoffer and start the transformation to becoming a more effective leader.

# Acknowledgement

I have I have many people to thank for their continuous support, mentoring, parenting and coaching throughout the writing and publishing of this book.

Thank you to Francis Mbunya, my book coach for the simplified structure, consistent feedback throughout the process and the necessary feedback I needed to keep writing. The start, writing and completion would not have been enjoyable without your help.

Special thanks to my parents, my brothers (could not have made it here without you), sisters in law (those powerful conversations) and my close circle (you know who you are) for the continuous support and for always asking "How is your book writing going?" This fueled my energy and passion to share my gift with my readers. You were just as excited as I was during the process. I could not wait to tell you when I completed each chapter. Thank you for making this a fun process.

Thank you to my business coach, Fabienne Raphael for helping me transform myself and my business to the fullest potential. I am grateful for the empowerment and the guidance to grow and keep impacting my clients' leadership journey.

Thank you to my mentors and specifically, Enid Dufresne Dario for showing me what authentic leadership is and for empowering me to lead in my truth. You said to me in your actions that it was okay to be me and lead authentically with my heart.

Thank you to my previous employers for the opportunity to lead and for the space to experience tremendous growth, the toughest moments and capture the best learnings. You gave me a gift that I am sharing with the world.

Thank you to my direct reports, peers and teams on my leadership journey. I could not have done it without you.

Thank you to my clients for deciding to do the work to lead more effectively. I am grateful to be part of your transformation.

Special thanks to my Aunty Rasie for always inspiring me to be the best I can be and to never stop moving forward. I have looked up to you since I knew I was named after you.

# About The Author

**Rasie** was born in Sierra Leone and lived there until she was 10 years old. Growing up with three brothers, mostly boy cousins, all she watched were action movies. When her parents were around, they watched Nigerian movies. Movies brought them together to one place and kept them connected. She will always cherish those moments.

She lived in the Gambia for a year before she got the opportunity to move to Canada. Moving to Canada was the most extreme change she went through yet. The climate, culture, relationships, and opportunities were simply different from Sierra Leone. She adapted quickly and made the most of the experience and the opportunities available to her.

She graduated from high school and was nominated grad of the year (it is an award given to the student that mostly represents the spirit of the graduating class by a majority vote). She was lost for words and forever grateful. While she was in high school, she worked part-time (30hrs per week) and played soccer and volleyball. She has always been driven to do more than what is expected of her. She did not know how to do things halfway; she had to always give her 100% and more.

Rasie's leadership journey started when she was in different sport teams and at her part-time job. It is something she has always enjoyed and most times, others looked at her to lead. Leading teams while she was employed at McDonald's, Starbucks and more, her leadership role was challenged frequently, and this kept her moving and impacting lives for the better. Her passion for people development and to be the best she can be will always be the driving force that pushed her towards achieving her goals. In her leadership journey, she had the opportunity to experience the following and more in the Operations Manager role:

- Reopen a McDonald's location

- Opened two Starbucks locations

- Reopened two Starbucks locations after the Fort McMurray Fires

- Hiring, training front of house staff for the Canucks Bar and Grill Opening.

- Received the Spirit of Starbucks Award.

- Lead teams from 20-80 people depending on the location.

- Built strong relationships with peers, employees, and customers.

She was married to Yusuff Bamigbade (RIP). Her late husband was her best friend and greatest ally. He always cheered her on to reach every single goal she aimed for. He was very patient and supportive of her early mornings and late nights of studying and working to reach her goals. He is deeply missed.

Rasie started her own coaching business, and she is enjoying every moment and is more than grateful for the challenges. You can say that she is very grounded, ambitious, and driven. When she believes that she can, she sure will. She is a leadership coach; coaching leaders to lead their lives and teams more effectively. Most clients she works with want to reach their goals sooner and enjoy the process with her expertise, experience, and coaching style.

Rasie believes that everything happens for us and we have the power to make a choice. She chooses to help others along her journey in life.

# Thank You for Reading

T hank you for taking the energy and time to capture what you need right now to jumpstart your authentic leadership journey. If there is one thing you take away, it is that there is always a way, and you have all the tools within you. For all my readers reading this to step into a higher level of energy in their leadership journey, I have a special gift for you. Go to www.rbjumpstartcoaching.com/ebookoffer to claim your special gift.

Manufactured by Amazon.ca
Bolton, ON

38424483R00061